THE SECRET SOCIETY OF MONSTER HUNTERS

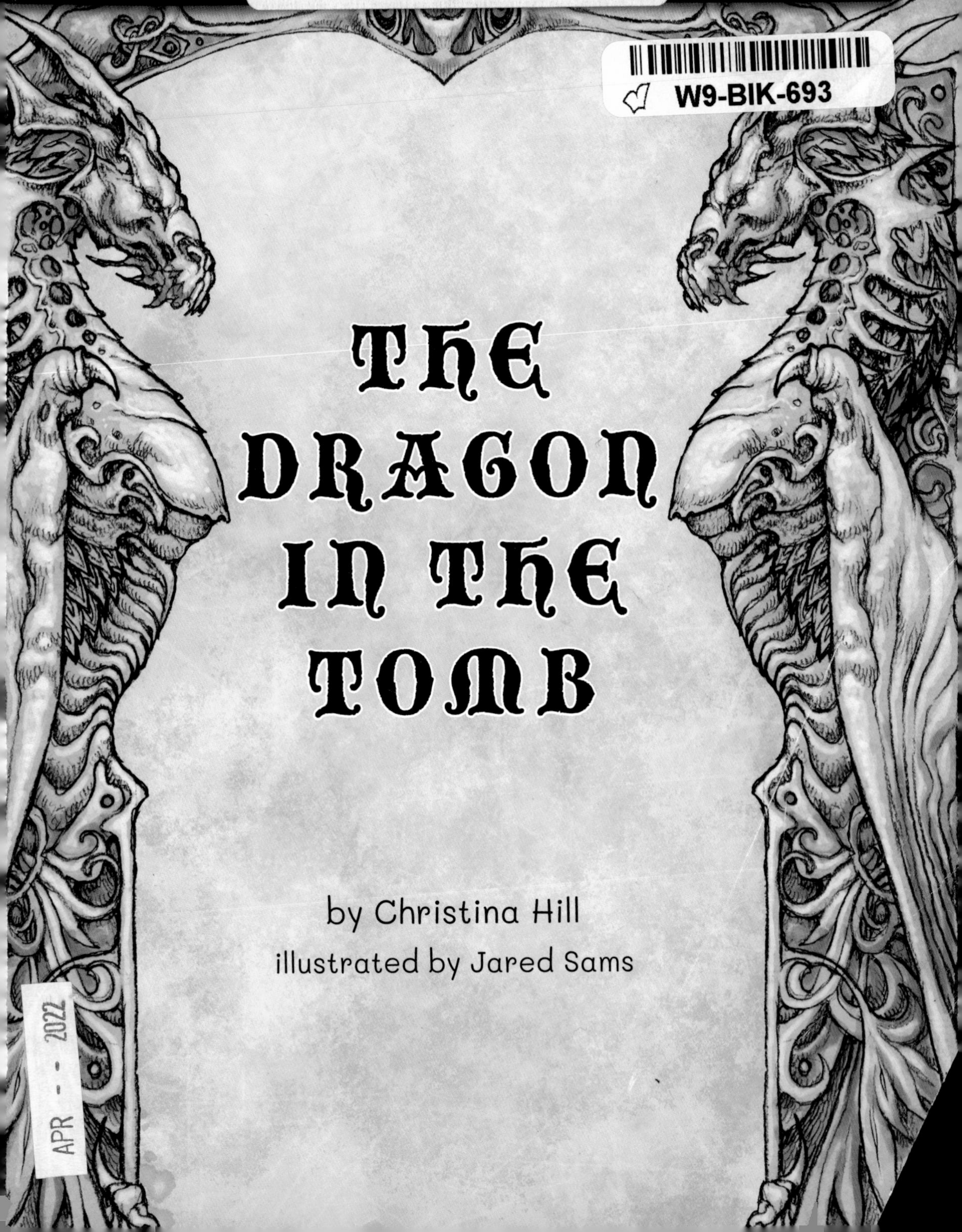

THE DRAGON IN THE TOMB

by Christina Hill

illustrated by Jared Sams

TORCH GRAPHIC PRESS

Published in the United States of America by Cherry Lake Publishing Group
Ann Arbor, Michigan
www.cherrylakepublishing.com

Reading Adviser: Beth Walker Gambro, MS, Ed., Reading Consultant, Yorkville, IL

Book Design: Book Buddy Media

Photo Credits: page 1: ©T Studio/Shutterstock; page 7: ©Pixabay(lined paper); page 7: ©estevez/ Shutterstock(background); page 7: ©John Lock/Shutterstock; page 9: ©aksol/Shutterstock; page 15: ©Alka5051/ Shutterstock; page 21: ©evgo1977/Shutterstock; page Background: ©Unholy Vault Designs/Shutterstock

Torch Graphic Press is an imprint of Cherry Lake Publishing Group.

Library of Congress Cataloging-in-Publication Data has been filed and is available at catalog.loc.gov

Cherry Lake Publishing Group would like to acknowledge the work of the Partnership for 21st Century Learning, a Network of Battelle for Kids. Please visit http://www.battelleforkids.org/networks/p21 for more information.

Printed in the United States of America
Corporate Graphics

TABLE OF CONTENTS

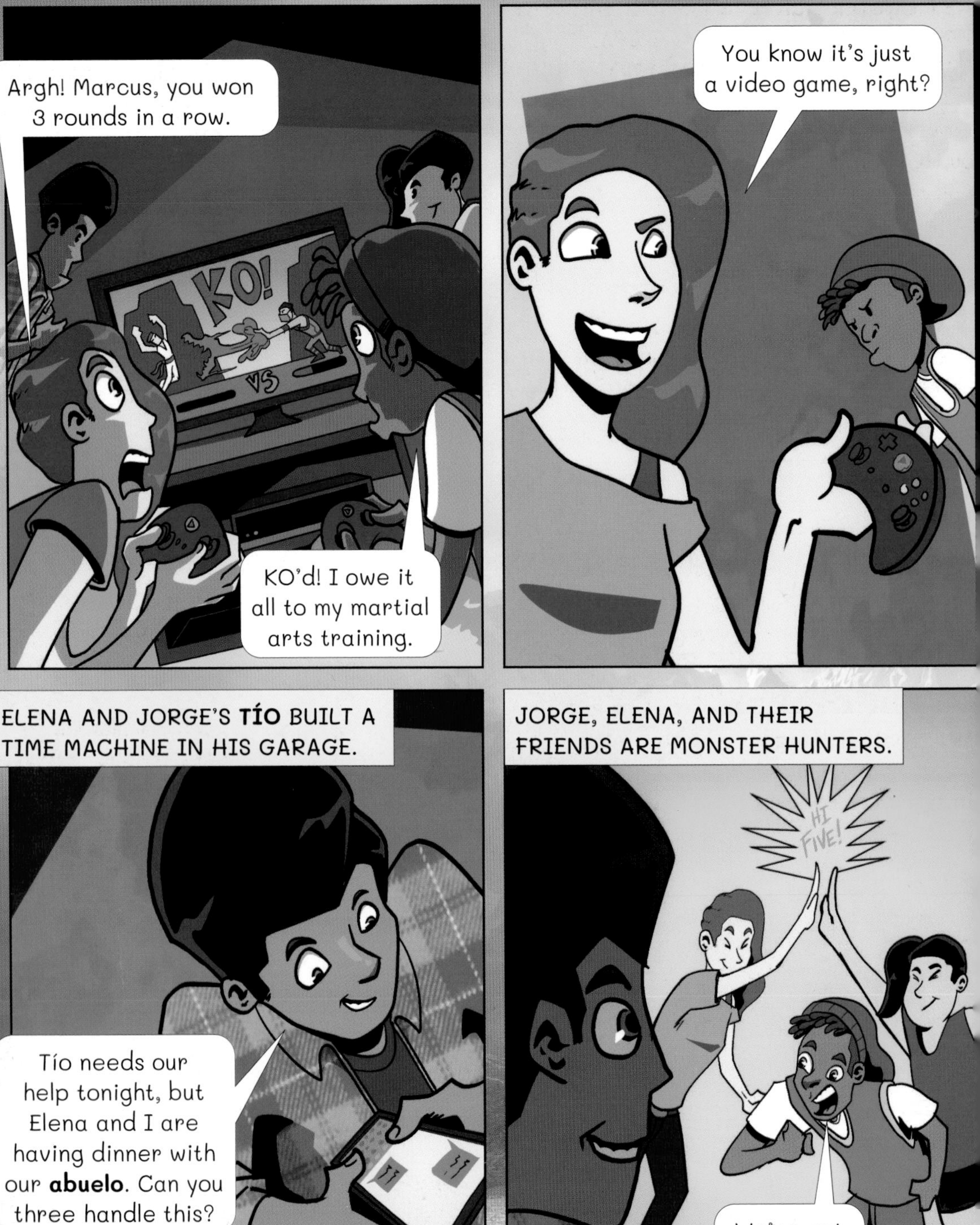
Argh! Marcus, you won 3 rounds in a row.
KO!
VS
KO'd! I owe it all to my martial arts training.
You know it's just a video game, right?
ELENA AND JORGE'S **TÍO** BUILT A TIME MACHINE IN HIS GARAGE.
Tío needs our help tonight, but Elena and I are having dinner with our **abuelo**. Can you three handle this?
JORGE, ELENA, AND THEIR FRIENDS ARE MONSTER HUNTERS.
HI FIVE!
We've got this, man!

tío: "uncle" in Spanish

abuelo: "grandfather" in Spanish

THE MONSTER HUNTERS TRAVEL THROUGH TIME TO KEEP THE MAGICAL WORLD SEPARATE FROM THE HUMAN WORLD.

Hey, kiddos! What do you think about taking a trip to ancient China?

Awesome! I've always wanted to go to China.

There are rumors of a dragon being used by a wicked emperor in ancient China. Your mission is to stop this from happening.

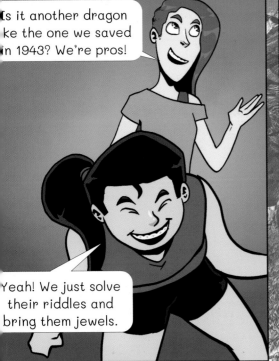

Is it another dragon like the one we saved in 1943? We're pros!

Yeah! We just solve their riddles and bring them jewels.

It's not like the Western dragon from last time. I learned about Chinese dragons in my martial arts class. They're symbols of power and luck.

DRAGON STYLE

Dragon-style kung fu is a fighting style. It resembles a dragon with its short flowing attacks.

Well, that just means this mission will be a piece of cake!

We're facing a good luck dragon? Easy peasy!

It won't be easy. Ancient China was a dangerous time, especially during the Qin dynasty.

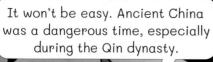

The Qin dynasty began in 259 BCE with the reign of Qin Shi Huang, also known as the Dragon Emperor.

Be careful and look out for each other. You only have 10 hours to complete this mission!

Don't worry! I'll keep them safe!

PACKING LIST

Clothing in ancient China changed in each dynasty. There were 13 dynasties in the history of China. Here was the style during the Qin dynasty:

* The emperor and nobility wore long silk robes in dark colors. This was unique to their dynasty. The emperor believed that dark colors represented water. Water was a symbol of power because it could extinguish fire.

* Common people wore linen robes and pants in lighter colors.

* The warrior class wore knee-length gowns over pants. Their armor was made out of leather and decorated with patterns.

* Long hair was the rage! Even men grew their hair long. Men's hair was usually worn in a flat bun. Women wore their hair up in 2 buns.

* Facial hair was admired. Men usually had some sort of facial hair. Many had long mustaches.

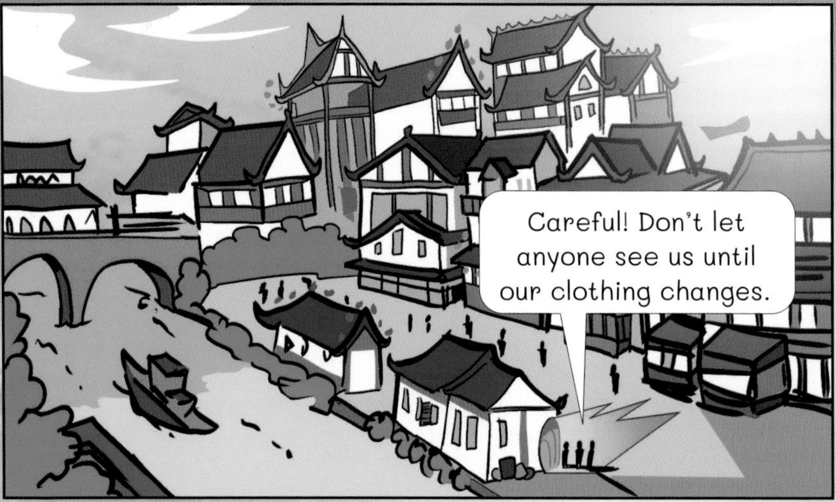
Careful! Don't let anyone see us until our clothing changes.

Chang'an was the ancient capital city of China. It was located in northern China and was surrounded by the Wei River, which made it a successful trading center.

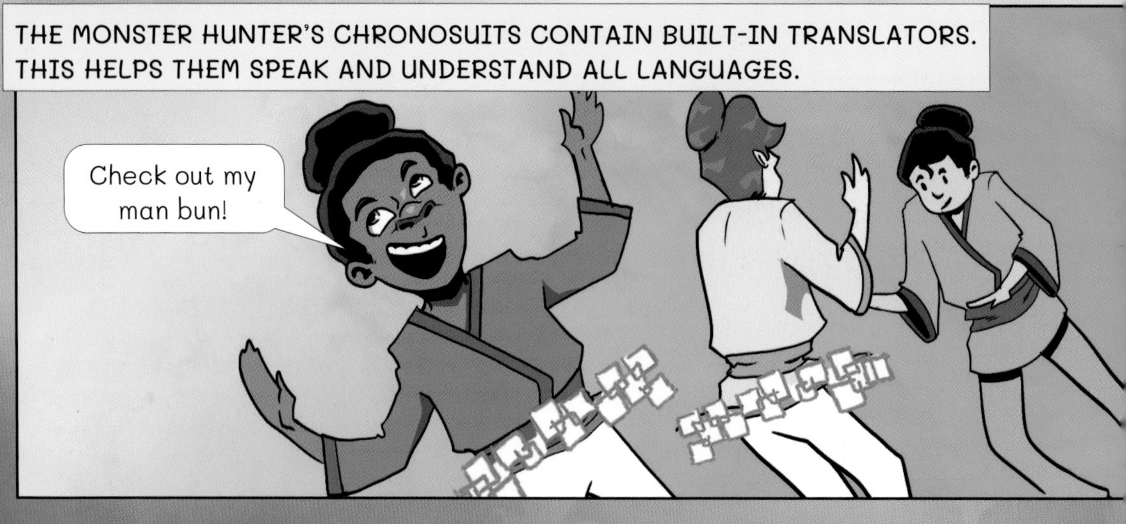
THE MONSTER HUNTER'S CHRONOSUITS CONTAIN BUILT-IN TRANSLATORS. THIS HELPS THEM SPEAK AND UNDERSTAND ALL LANGUAGES.
Check out my man bun!

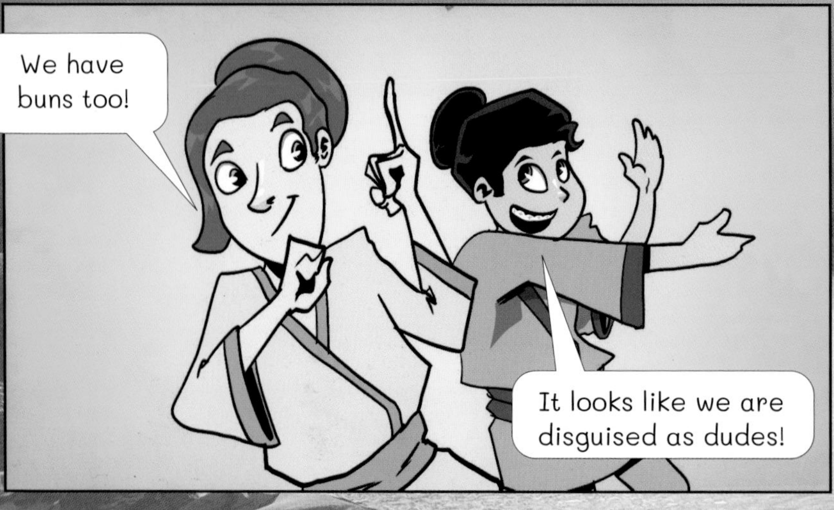
We have buns too!
It looks like we are disguised as dudes!

In ancient China, women were not allowed to work outside of the home or in the marketplace.

TIPS FOR THE TIME PERIOD

* The Qin dynasty was the first to unify China under one ruler. Construction on the Great Wall of China began. The Great Wall was meant to keep China safe from invaders.

* Emperor Qin created a standard form of currency and writing for the first time in China.

* Ancient China had a strict social **hierarchy**. This meant that people were ranked by their place in society.

    * Top rank: emperor, soldiers, and nobles

    * Low rank: merchants, farmers, and craftsmen

    * Lowest rank: slaves

* Jobs and roles were inherited from parents. But sometimes it was possible to move to a higher rank.

* During the Qin dynasty, peasants worked as farmers. They also harvested silk for the nobility's clothing. They helped to build roads and canals to increase trade.

* Many of the festivals celebrated in China today come from ancient times.

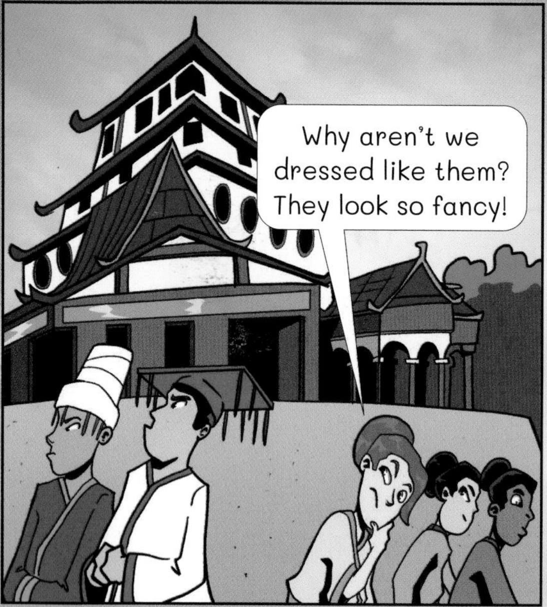
Why aren't we dressed like them? They look so fancy!

People in ancient China wore clothing to represent their social class.

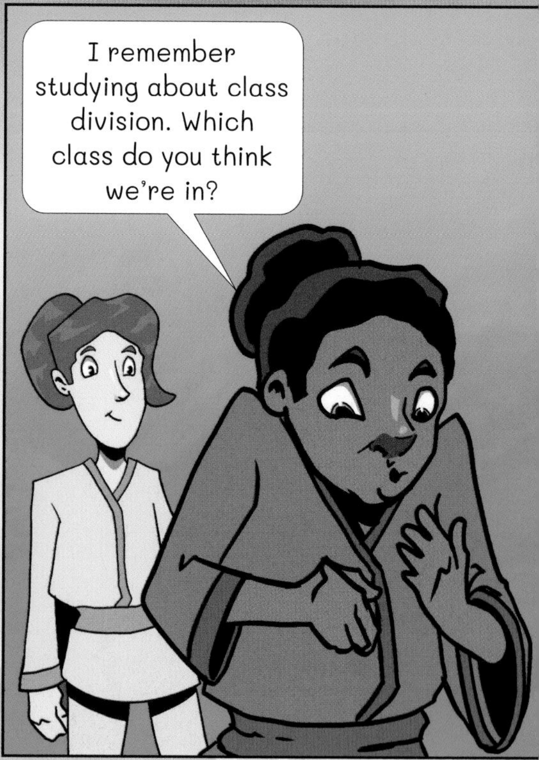
I remember studying about class division. Which class do you think we're in?

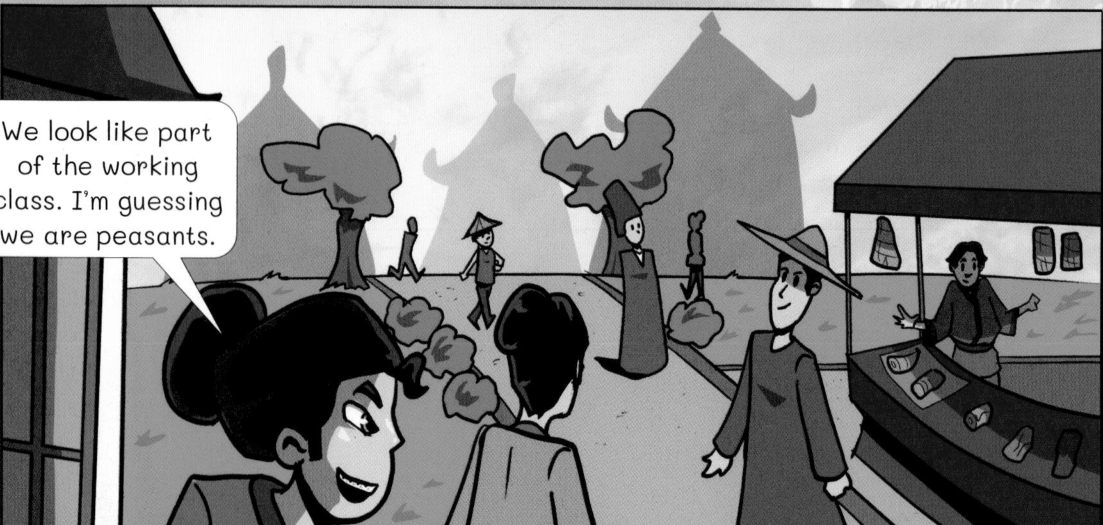
We look like part of the working class. I'm guessing we are peasants.

Peasants could be punished if they wore silk clothing.

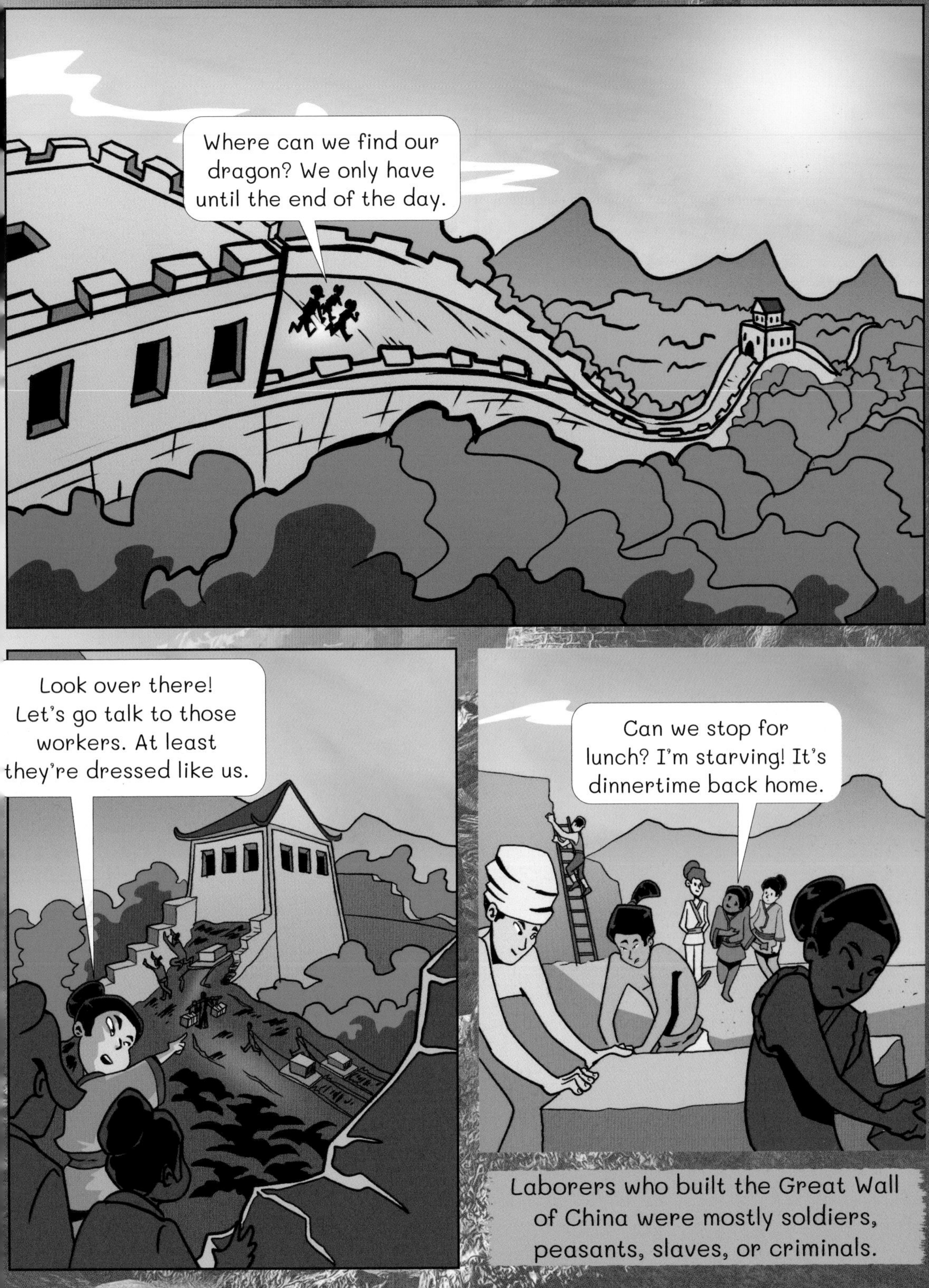
Where can we find our dragon? We only have until the end of the day.
Look over there! Let's go talk to those workers. At least they're dressed like us.
Can we stop for lunch? I'm starving! It's dinnertime back home.
Laborers who built the Great Wall of China were mostly soldiers, peasants, slaves, or criminals.

Let's join them and see what we can learn about the dragon.

It's hot! And we're supposed to be finding a dragon, not building a wall. This is hard work.

Construction on the Great Wall of China lasted for 2,000 years. The wall stretches across over 13,000 miles (20,922 kilometers) of land.

It's not that heavy!

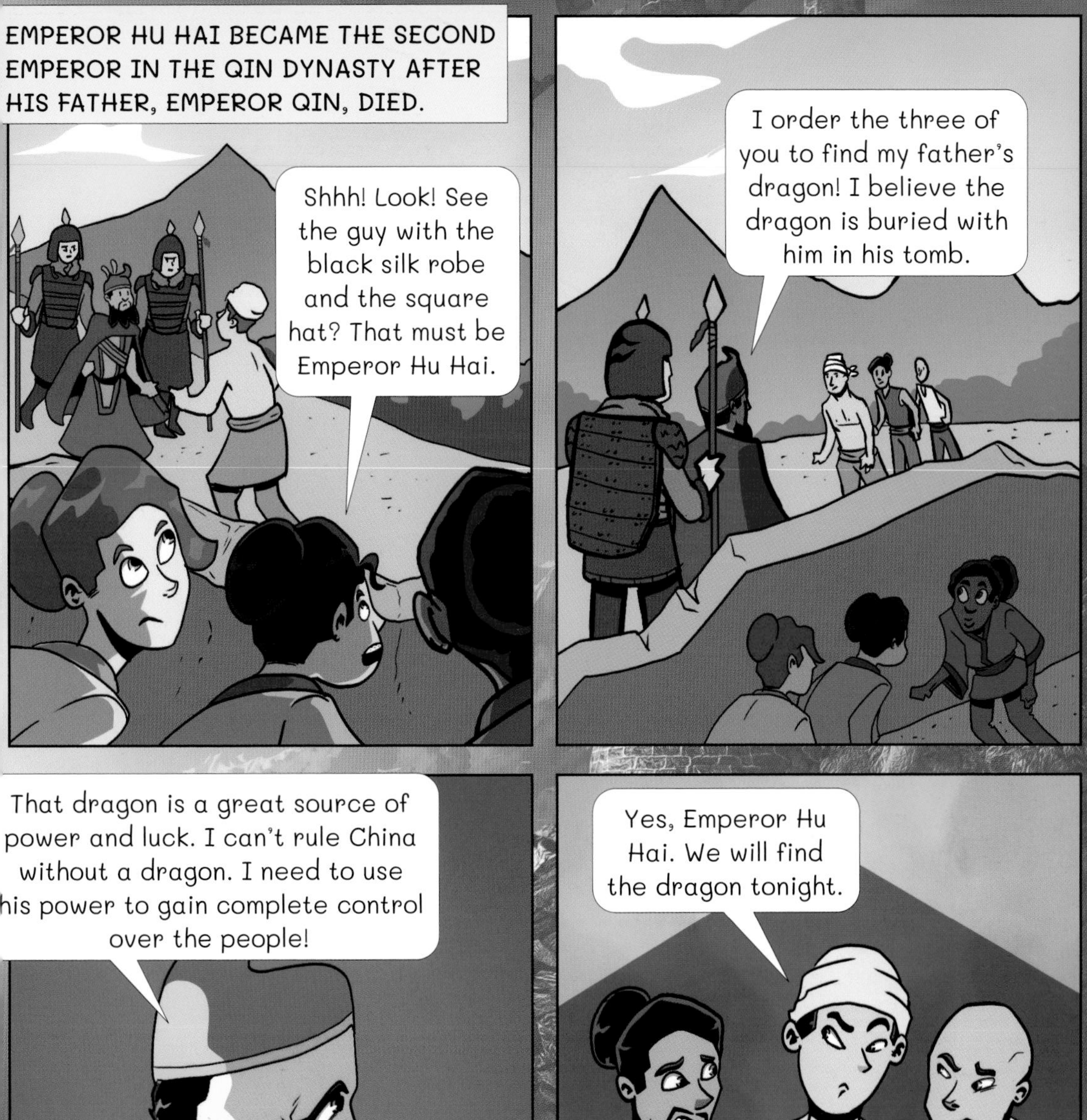
EMPEROR HU HAI BECAME THE SECOND EMPEROR IN THE QIN DYNASTY AFTER HIS FATHER, EMPEROR QIN, DIED.
Shhh! Look! See the guy with the black silk robe and the square hat? That must be Emperor Hu Hai.
I order the three of you to find my father's dragon! I believe the dragon is buried with him in his tomb.
That dragon is a great source of power and luck. I can't rule China without a dragon. I need to use his power to gain complete control over the people!
Yes, Emperor Hu Hai. We will find the dragon tonight.

The dragon was the symbol of Emperor Qin's authority. His people believed that he **descended** from the dragon's bloodline.

descended: came from a specific group or ancestor

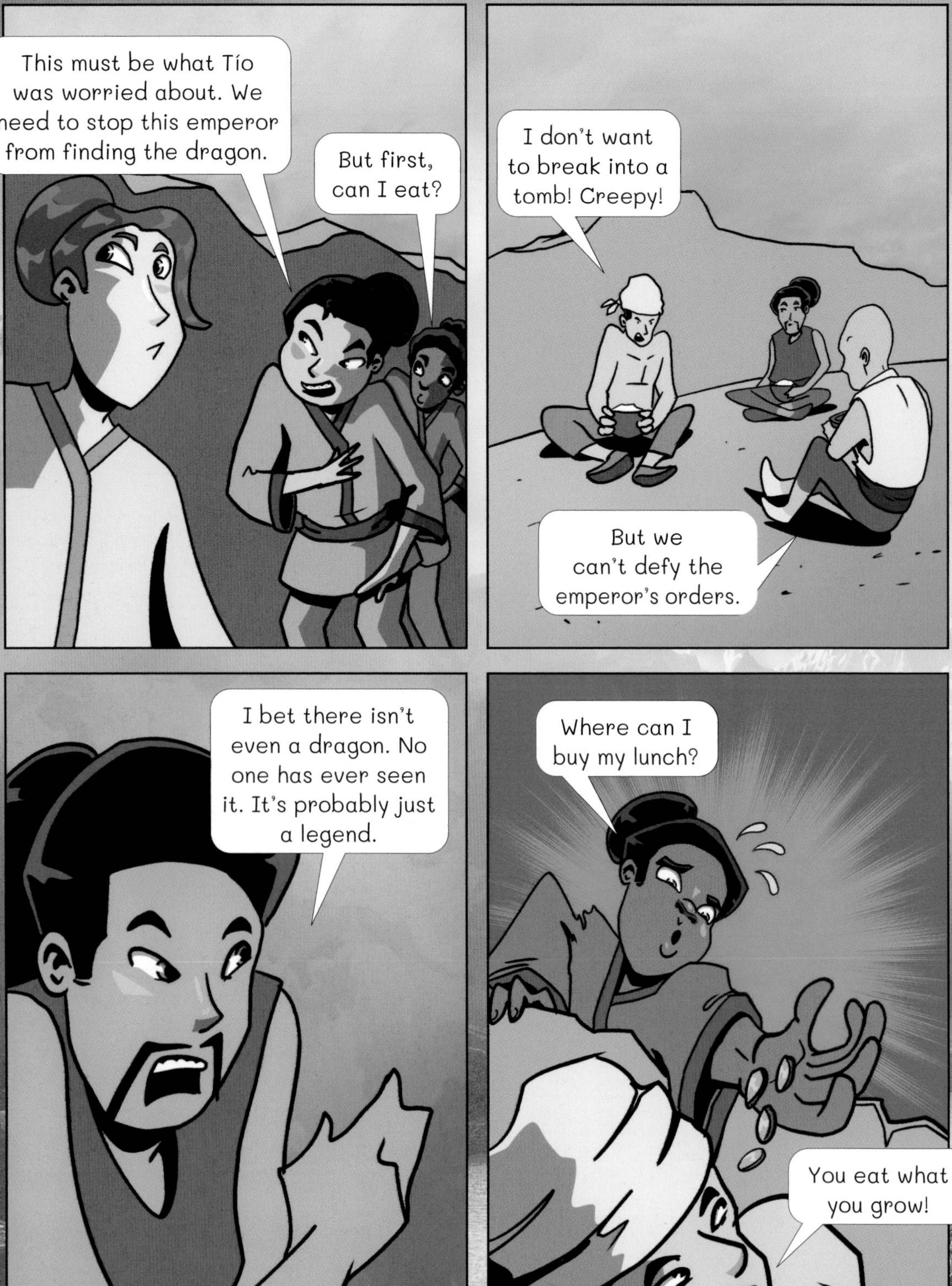
This must be what Tío was worried about. We need to stop this emperor from finding the dragon.
But first, can I eat?
I don't want to break into a tomb! Creepy!
But we can't defy the emperor's orders.
I bet there isn't even a dragon. No one has ever seen it. It's probably just a legend.
Where can I buy my lunch?
You eat what you grow!

WHAT IS A CHINESE DRAGON?

Do not confuse Chinese dragons with Western ones! Western dragons breathe fire, play mind games, and speak in riddles. Chinese dragons are quite different!

* Chinese dragons can take on many forms. Some look like turtles or fish. But most often they are serpentlike creatures with 4 legs.

* Chinese dragons have 117 scales.

* Chinese dragons do not have wings. They can soar through the air using magic.

* They are believed to have special control over water and the weather.

* Chinese dragons are symbols of luck, strength, and power.

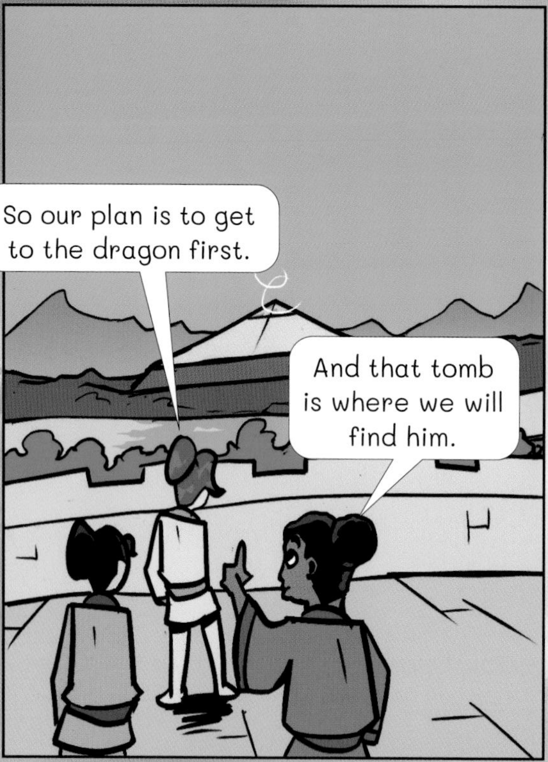
So our plan is to get to the dragon first.
And that tomb is where we will find him.

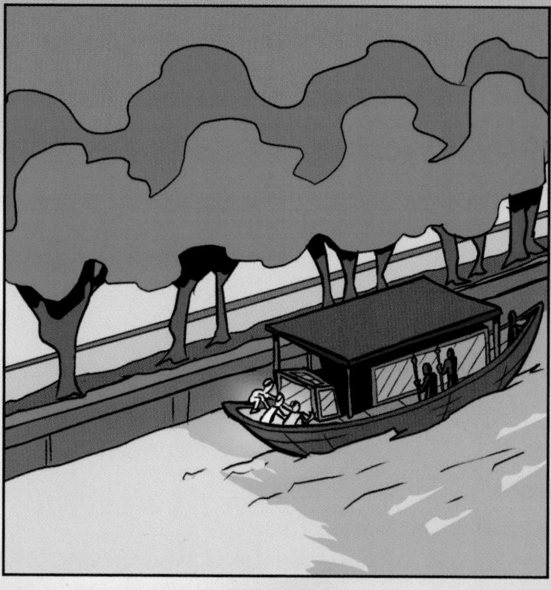

Ancient China had a vast system of canals. The Qin dynasty was the first to connect the Xiang and Li Rivers.

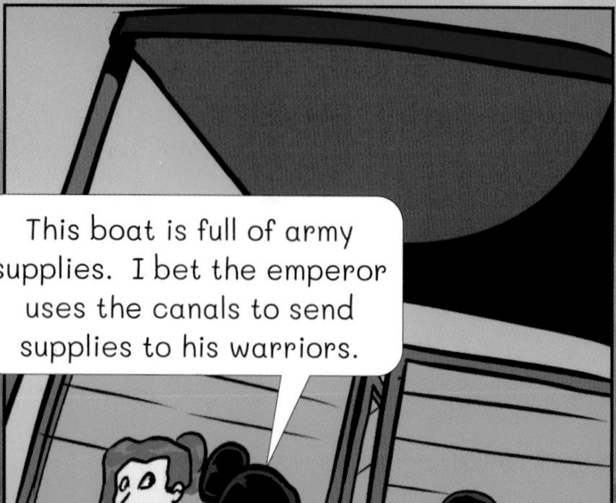
This boat is full of army supplies. I bet the emperor uses the canals to send supplies to his warriors.

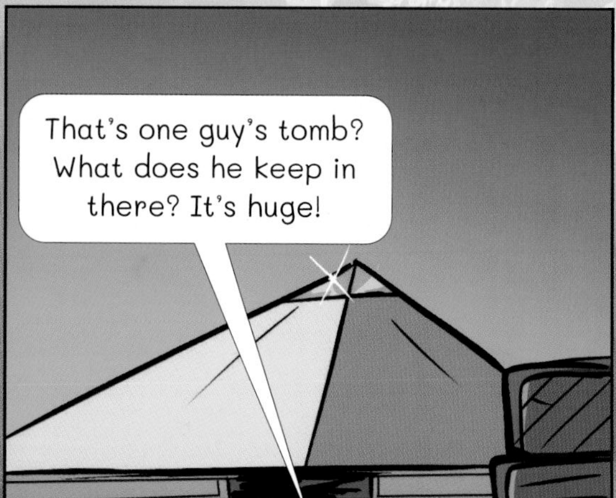
That's one guy's tomb? What does he keep in there? It's huge!

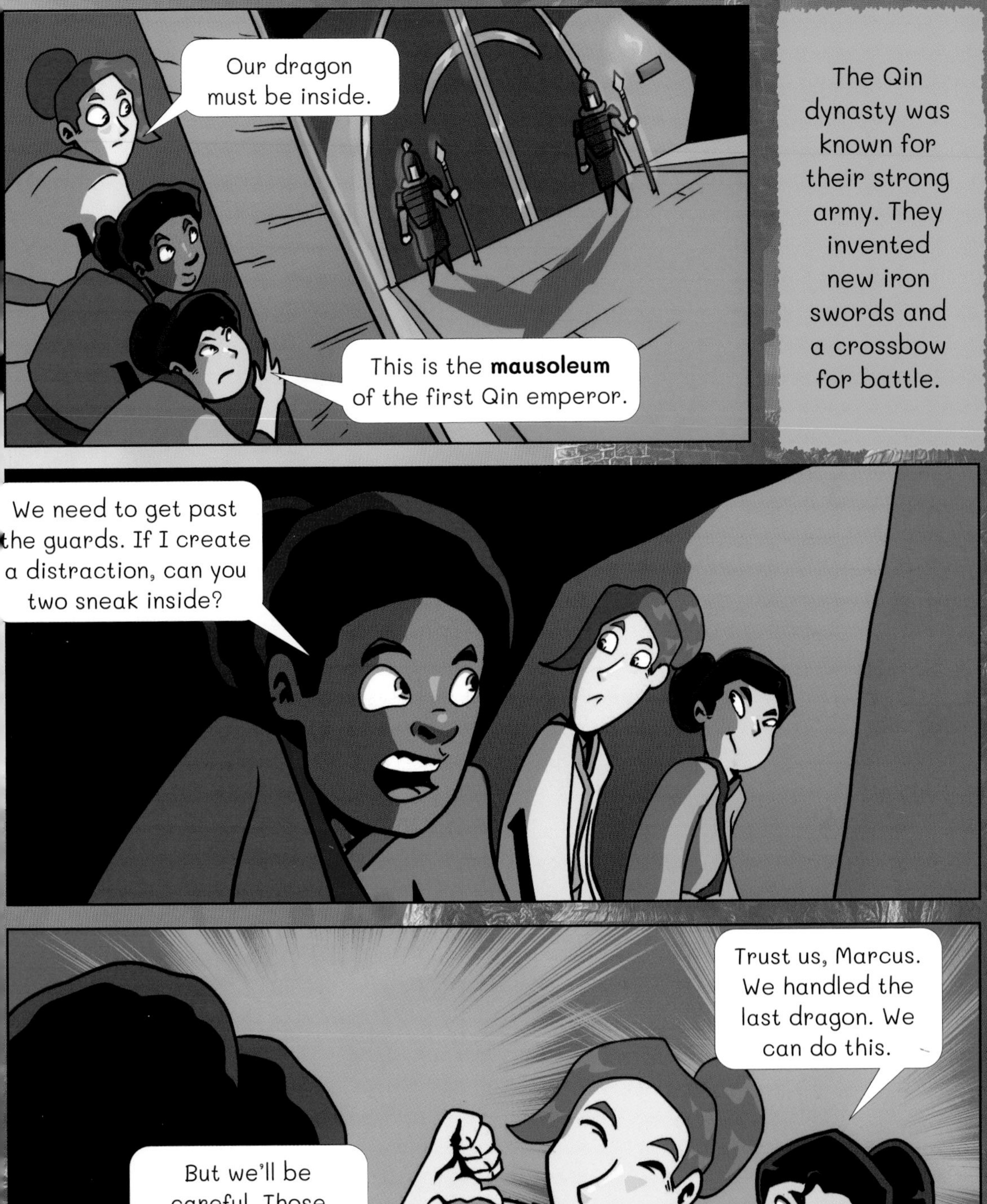
Our dragon must be inside.
This is the **mausoleum** of the first Qin emperor.
The Qin dynasty was known for their strong army. They invented new iron swords and a crossbow for battle.
We need to get past the guards. If I create a distraction, can you two sneak inside?
Trust us, Marcus. We handled the last dragon. We can do this.
But we'll be careful. Those guards look tough!

mausoleum: a large burial place or building

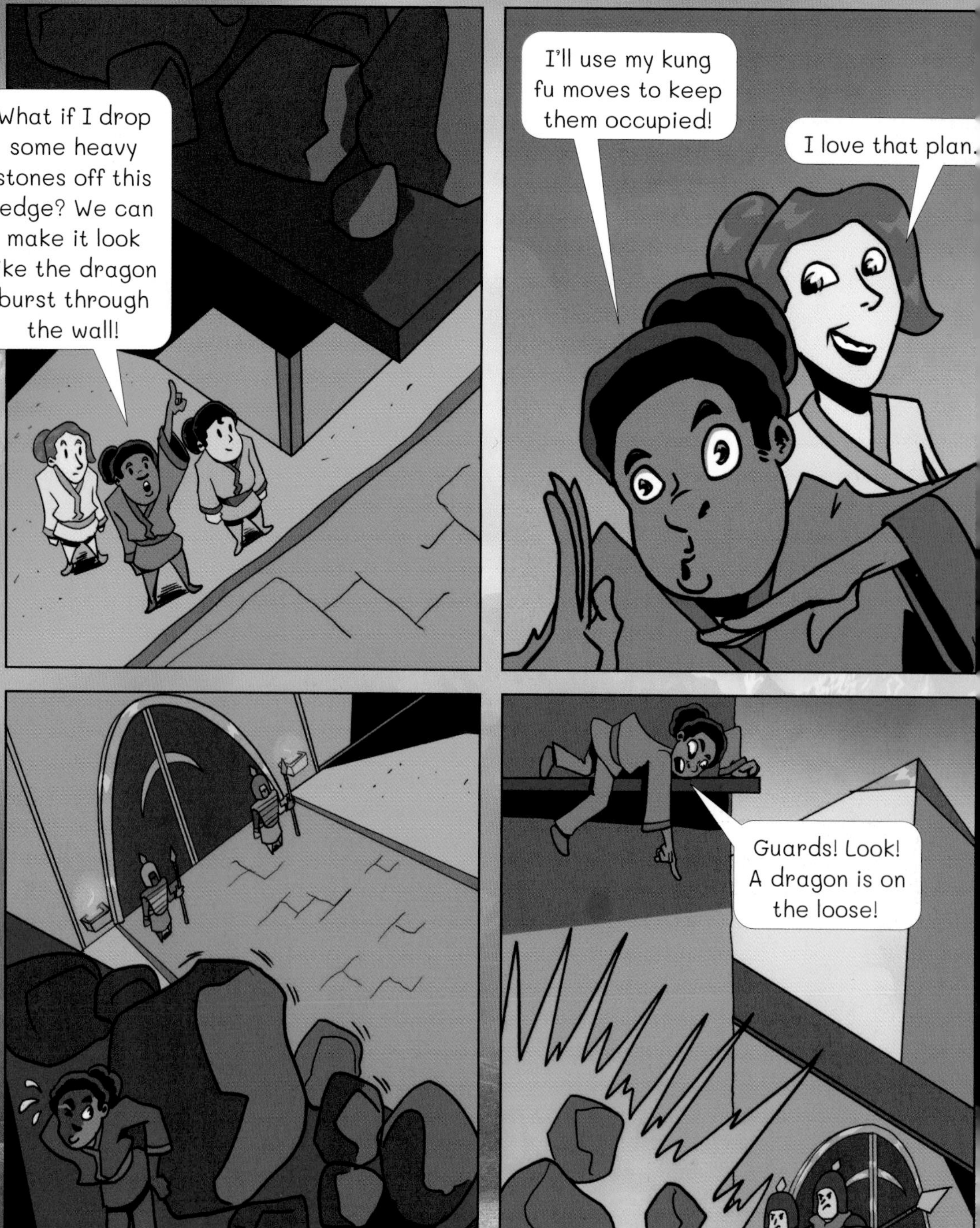
What if I drop some heavy stones off this ledge? We can make it look like the dragon burst through the wall!
I'll use my kung fu moves to keep them occupied!
I love that plan.
Guards! Look! A dragon is on the loose!

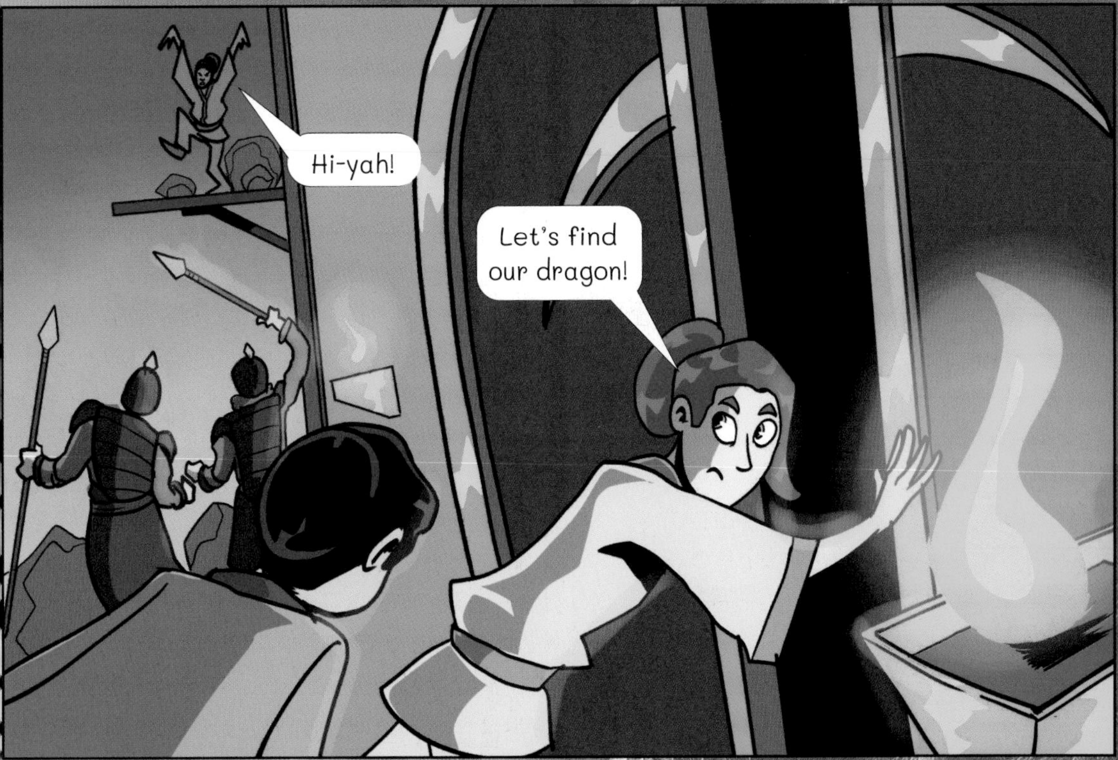
Hi-yah!
Let's find our dragon!

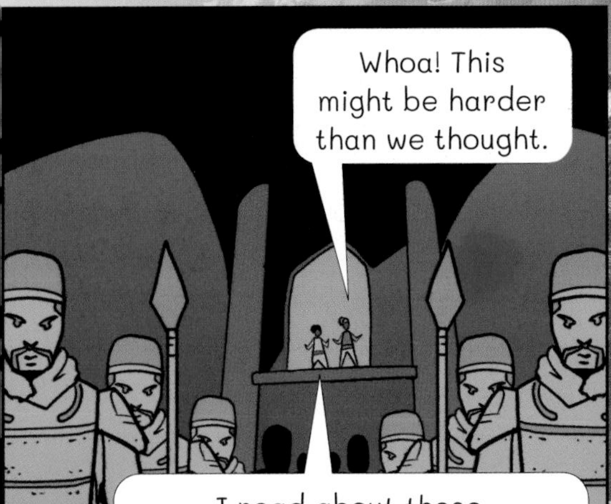
Whoa! This might be harder than we thought.
I read about these **terracotta** soldiers! I think Emperor Qin wanted to protect his spirit after he died.

There are more than 8,000 terracotta soldiers in the mausoleum. There are also terracotta acrobats, animals, horses, and chariots.

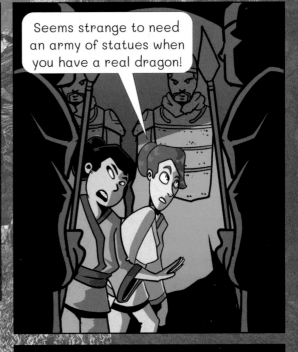

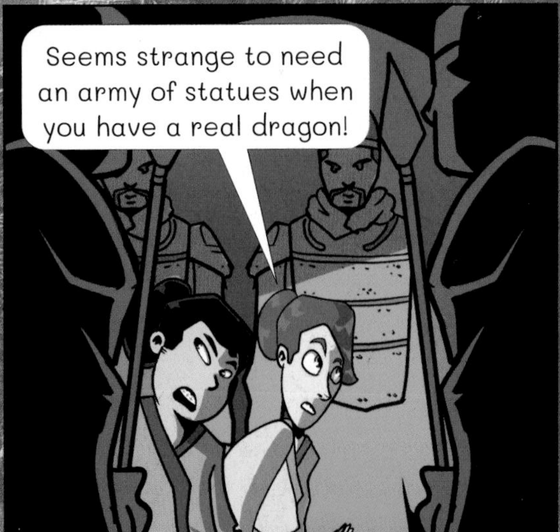
Seems strange to need an army of statues when you have a real dragon!

terracotta: a hard brownish-red clay used to make sculptures

Stand back, Amy. We aren't exactly sure if the dragon is nice!

It's probably just like a big dog. Here, dragon, dragon, dragon!

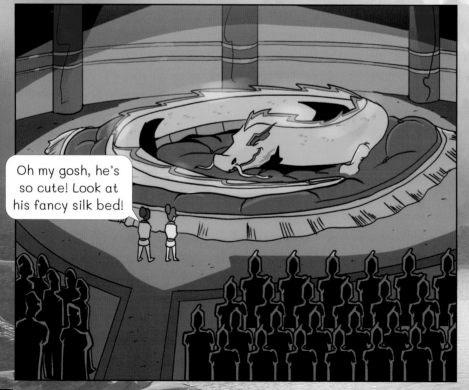

Oh my gosh, he's so cute! Look at his fancy silk bed!

Silk was in high demand. China dominated the trade market. They kept their silk-making process a secret for 1,000 years!

SURVIVAL TIPS

While Chinese dragons are considered to be kind and loving creatures, they are still powerful! Here are some tips to help you if you encounter a Chinese dragon.

* Do not threaten the dragon. It is not aggressive by nature. But if it's **provoked**, it may lash out.

* Remember that dragons can control water. Try to avoid places where the dragon could cause a flood.

* Dragons have 1 rival animal—the tiger! If you have a pet tiger, you surely will be safe around a Chinese dragon.

* Most likely, you won't need any of these tips and your encounter will be peaceful. Offer to be the dragon's friend, and you will be safe. Back scratches can help!

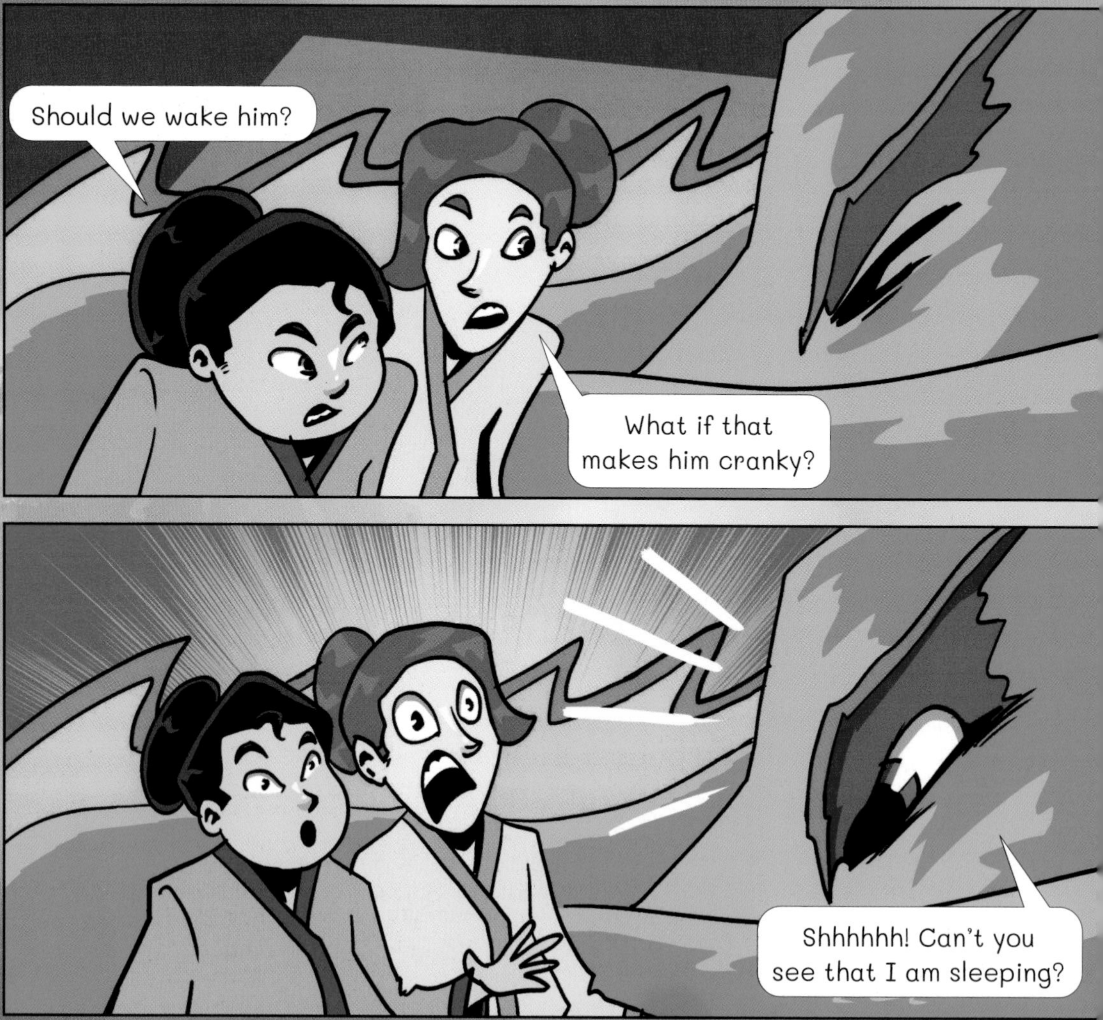
Should we wake him?
What if that makes him cranky?
Shhhhhh! Can't you see that I am sleeping?

Ancient China was full of legends and tales of magic. Emperor Qin died on an **expedition**. He was looking for a magic potion that would help him live forever.

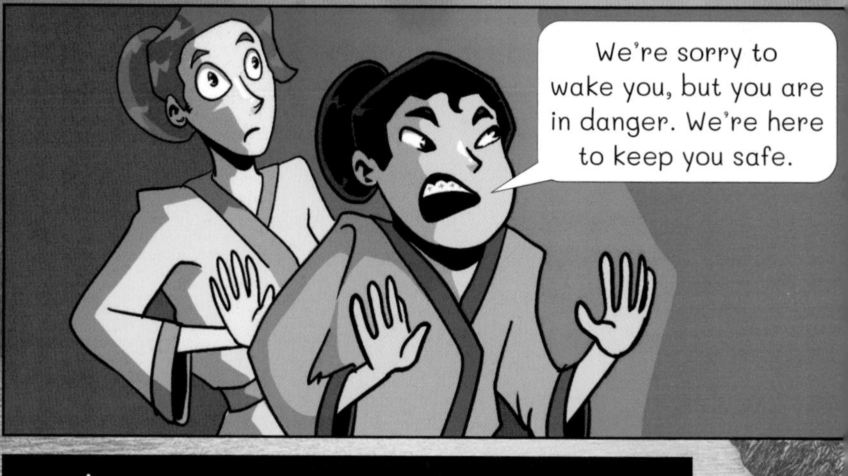
We're sorry to wake you, but you are in danger. We're here to keep you safe.

expedition: a journey or trip with a specific purpose

Let me get this straight. You two are here to keep me safe? Safe from what? Thousands of statues?

The new emperor thinks having a dragon will give him control over the people. We think he wants to use your powers for evil.

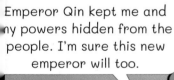

Emperor Qin kept me and my powers hidden from the people. I'm sure this new emperor will too.

We don't think Emperor Hu Hai has good **motives**. We need to keep you safely hidden from him.

Sorry, but I am not leaving this tomb. Just look at this bed! It's so comfy. It's made of the finest Chinese silk.

SNUGGLE SNUG

24

zongzi
rice du

motives: the goals of

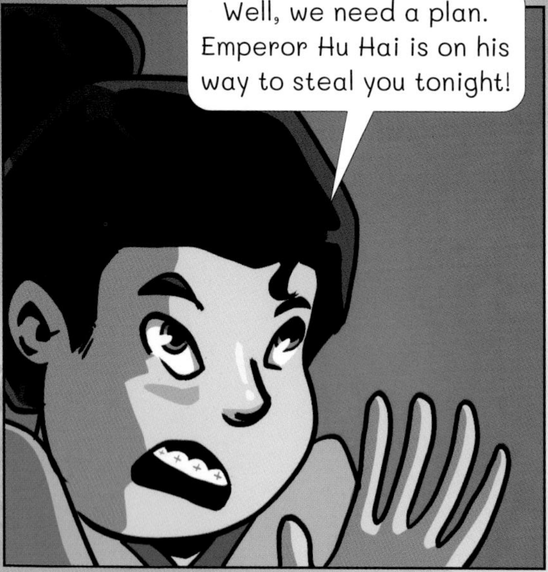
Well, we need a plan. Emperor Hu Hai is on his way to steal you tonight!

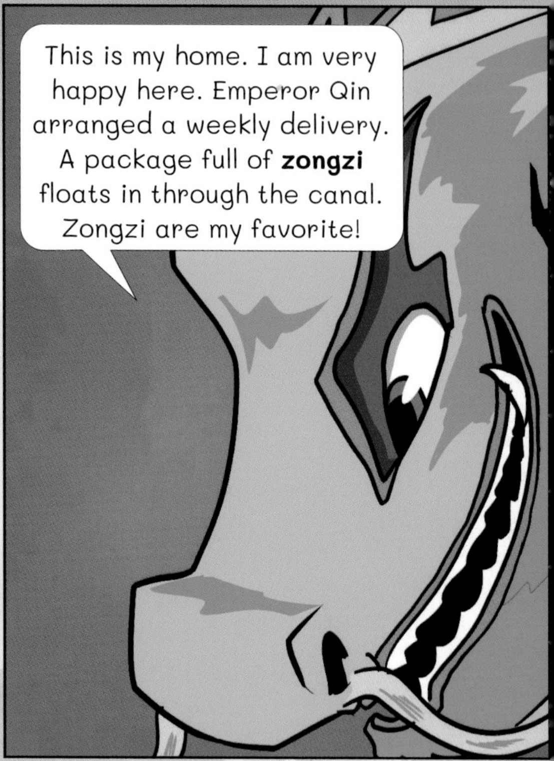
This is my home. I am very happy here. Emperor Qin arranged a weekly delivery. A package full of **zongzi** floats in through the canal. Zongzi are my favorite!

Hu Hai took over the throne by forging a letter pretending to be his father. He sent the letter to his older brother. The letter ordered him to die.

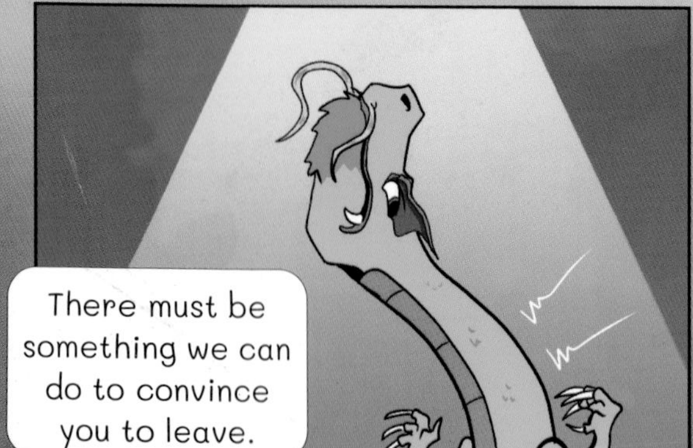
There must be something we can do to convince you to leave.
There is something. Scratch my back! My scales are so itchy.

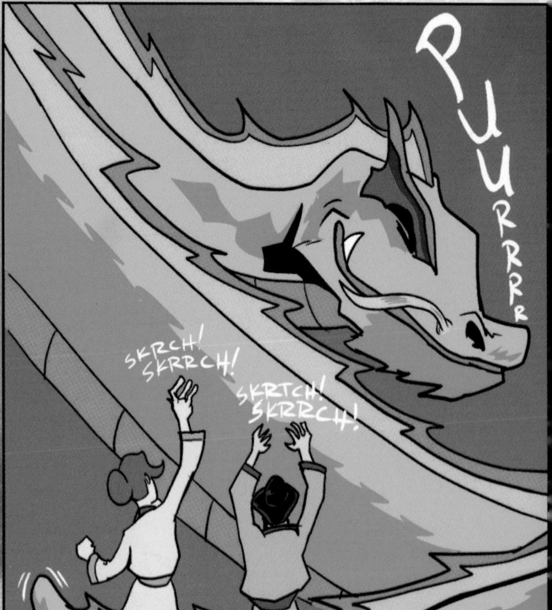
PUURRRRR
SKRCH! SKRRCH!
SKRTCH! SKRRCH!

: a traditional sticky
mpling

Whoa! Looks like you found the dragon.

These are the best back scratches I've ever had.

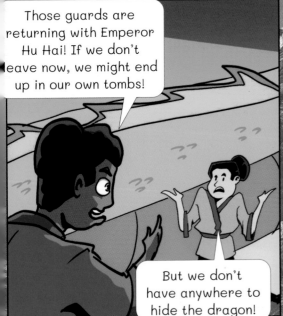

Those guards are returning with Emperor Hu Hai! If we don't leave now, we might end up in our own tombs!

But we don't have anywhere to hide the dragon!

The Chinese word for tornado means "dragon twisting wind."

I promise to stay hidden in this room if you move my comfy bed in here. If I hear anyone come, I will **summon** a tornado.

summon: to command or create

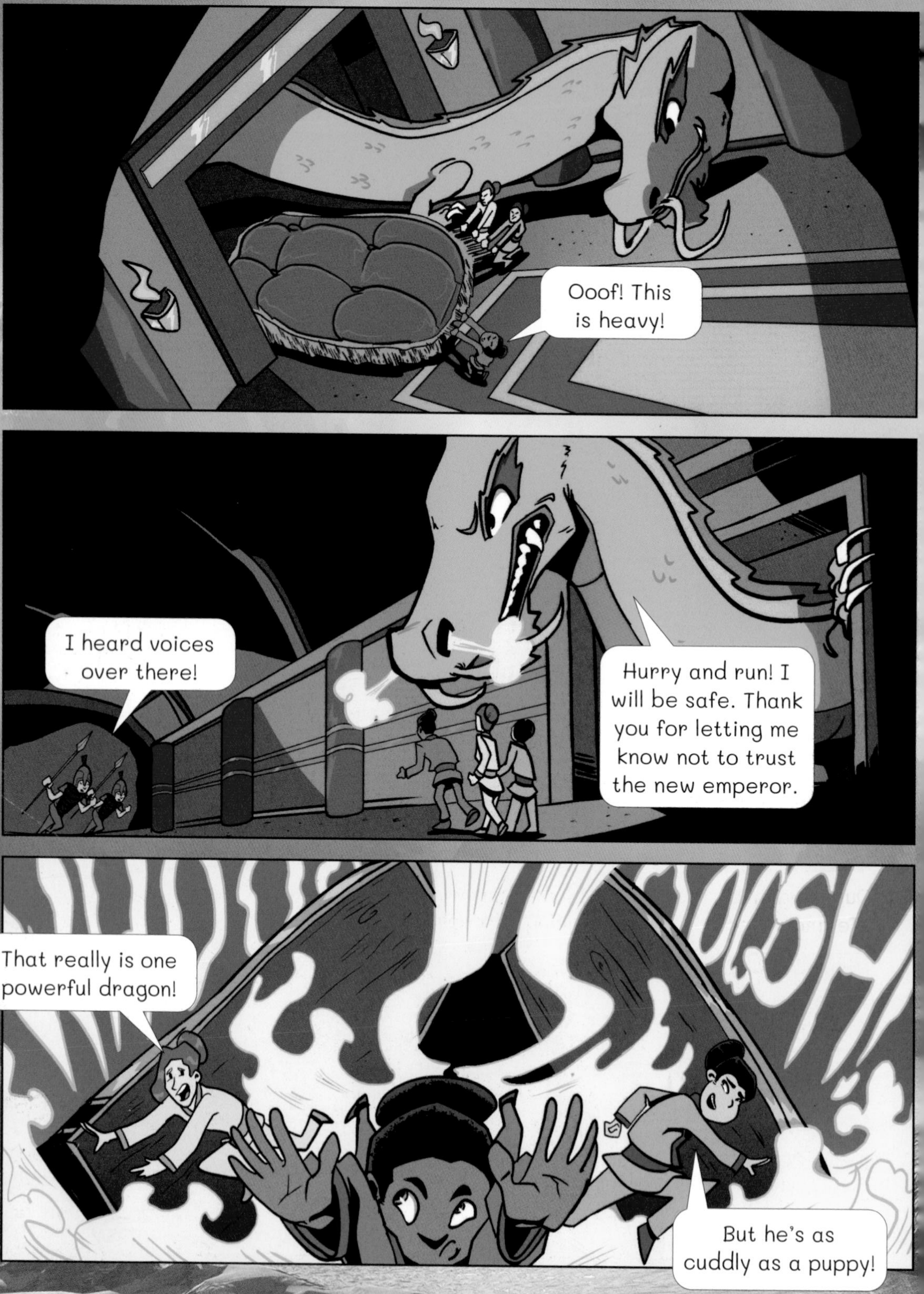
Ooof! This is heavy!
I heard voices over there!
Hurry and run! I will be safe. Thank you for letting me know not to trust the new emperor.
That really is one powerful dragon!
But he's as cuddly as a puppy!

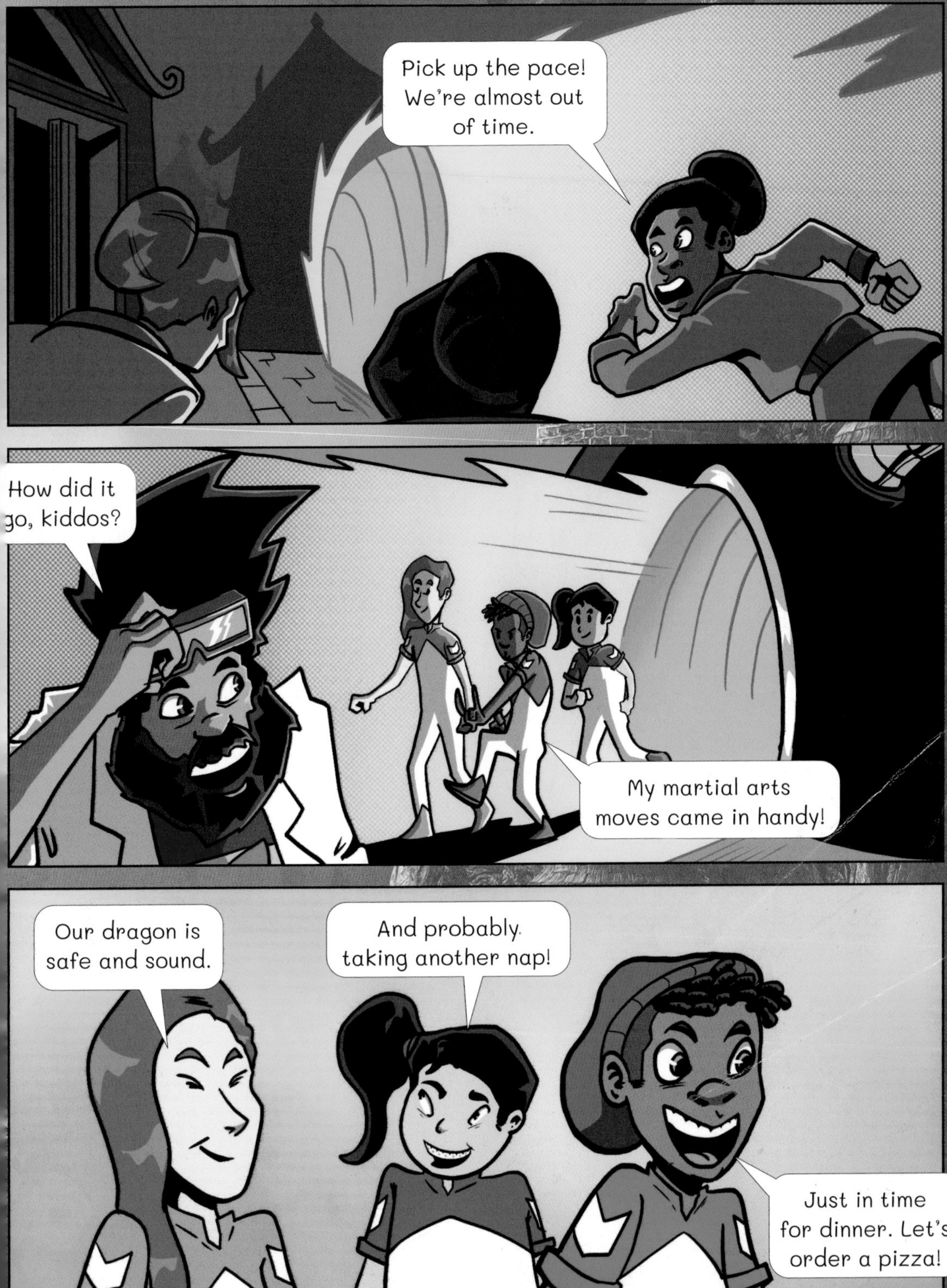
Pick up the pace! We're almost out of time.
How did it go, kiddos?
My martial arts moves came in handy!
Our dragon is safe and sound.
And probably taking another nap!
Just in time for dinner. Let's order a pizza!

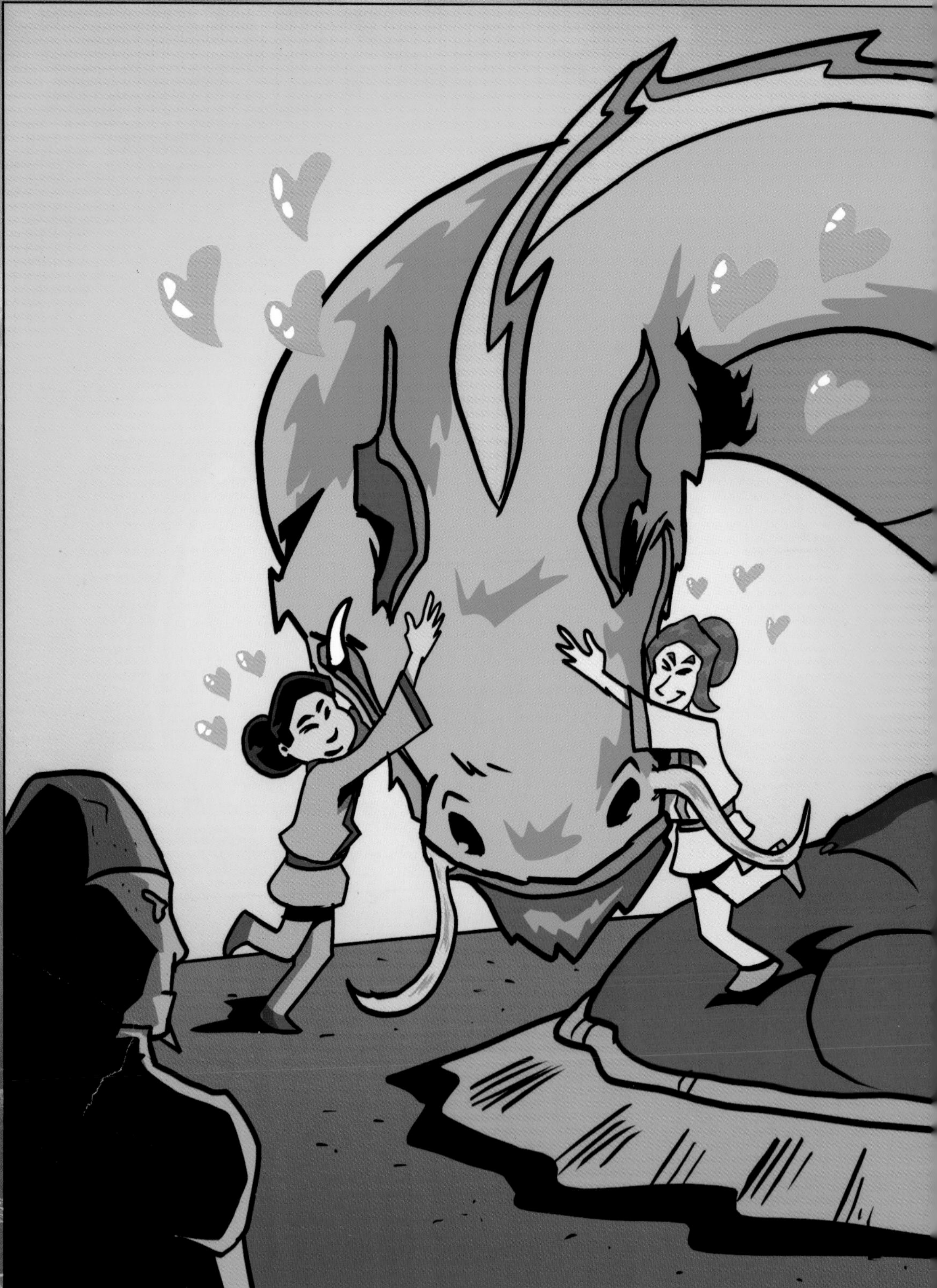

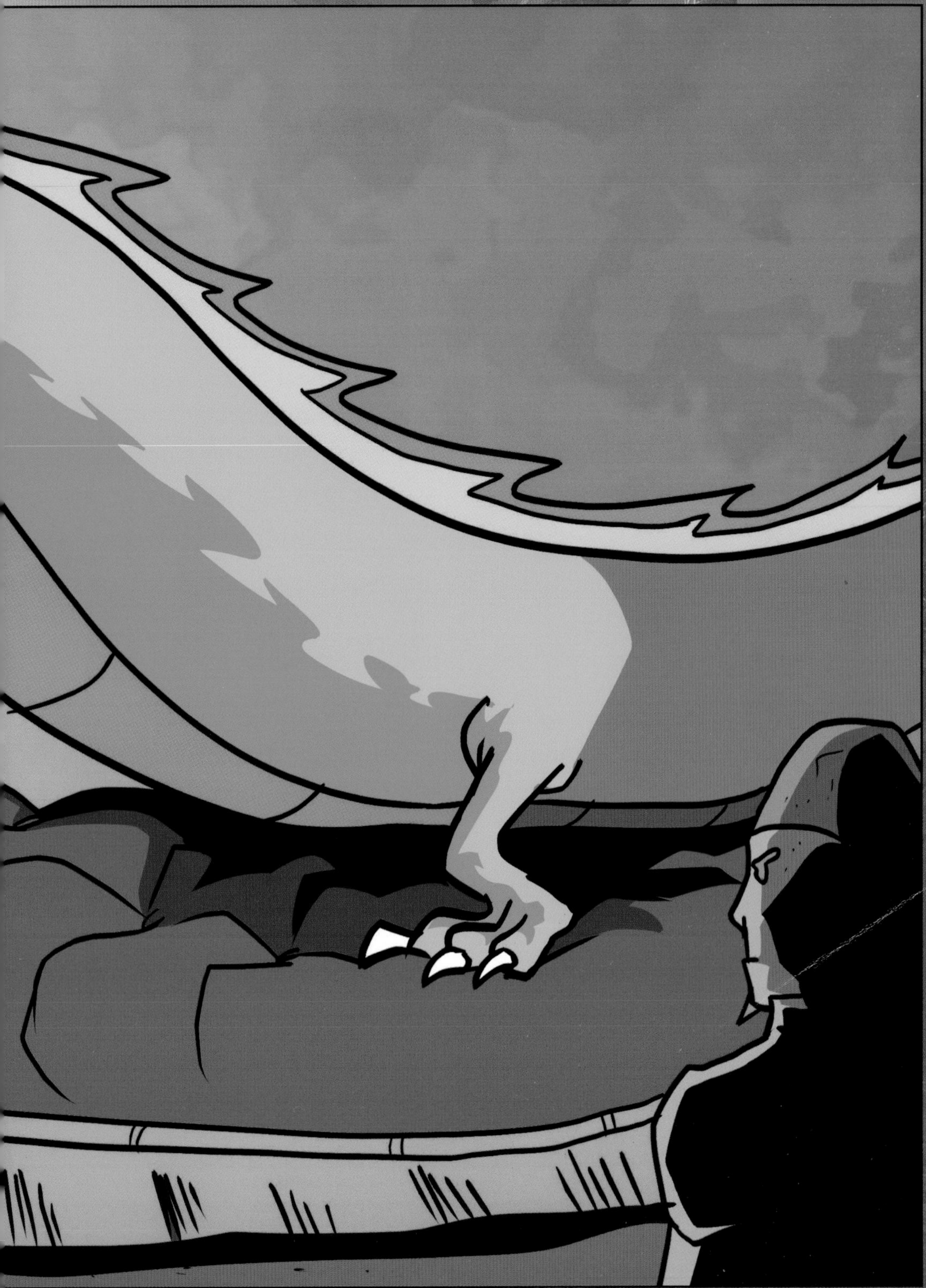

DESIGN A BLUEPRINT

A blueprint is what **architects** use to plan a new building design. It is a map of how they want their building to look.

Think about Emperor Qin's tomb. This is a real place in China. It was discovered by farmers who were digging a well in 1974. Today it is a protected site. The tomb section of the mausoleum has never been opened. **Archaeologists** think they don't have the right technology to open it. They do not want to damage the tomb. What lies behind the tomb walls? It remains a mystery!

Materials:

* paper   * pen or pencil

Instructions:

Draw a blueprint to show what you imagine the uncovered tomb looks like. Keep in mind the following as you draw your design:

* Is it a maze of tunnels?

* Are there canals full of water?

* What is buried with the emperor? Precious jewels?

* Include multiple entrances and exit points.

* Most importantly: Don't forget to include a dragon house!

architects: people who design and create buildings

archaeologists: people who study human history, usually through excavation

LEARN MORE

BOOKS

Kovacs, Vic. *The Culture of the Qin and Han Dynasties of China.* New York, NY: The Rosen Publishing Group, Inc., 2016.

Professor Beaver. *Ancient China's Inventions, Technology, and Engineering.* Newark, DE: Speedy Publishing, LLC, 2017.

WEBSITES

Ducksters—Ancient China
https://www.ducksters.com/history/china/ancient_china.php

DK Find Out—Ancient China
https://www.dkfindout.com/us/history/ancient-china

THE MONSTER HUNTER TEAM

JORGE
TÍO HECTOR'S NEPHEW, JORGE, LOVES MUSIC. AT 16 HE IS ONE OF THE OLDEST MONSTER HUNTERS AND LEADER OF THE GROUP.

MARCUS
MARCUS IS 14 AND IS WISE BEYOND HIS YEARS. HE IS A PROBLEM SOLVER, OFTEN GETTING THE GROUP OUT OF STICKY SITUATIONS.

FIONA
FIONA IS FIERCE AND PROTECTIVE. AT 16 SHE IS A ROLLER DERBY CHAMPION AND IS ONE OF JORGE'S CLOSEST FRIENDS.

ELENA
ELENA IS JORGE'S LITTLE SISTER AND TÍO HECTOR'S NIECE. AT 14, SHE IS THE HEART AND SOUL OF THE GROUP. ELENA IS KIND, THOUGHTFUL, AND SINCERE.

AMY
AMY IS 15. SHE LOVES BOOKS AND HISTORY. AMY AND ELENA SPEND ALMOST EVERY WEEKEND TOGETHER. THEY ARE ATTACHED AT THE HIP.

TÍO HECTOR
JORGE AND ELENA'S TÍO IS THE MASTERMIND BEHIND THE MONSTER HUNTERS. HIS TIME TRAVEL MACHINE MAKES IT ALL POSSIBLE.

GLOSSARY

abuelo (uh-BWEI-low) "grandfather" in Spanish

archaeologists (ahr-kee-AH-luh-jists) people who study human history, usually through excavation

architects (AHR-ki-tekts) people who design and create buildings

descended (dih-SEND-ed) came from a specific group or ancestor

expedition (ek-spi-DISH-uhn) a journey or trip with a specific purpose

hierarchy (HAHY-uh-rahr-kee) a system in which people are ranked one above another

mausoleum (maw-suh-LEE-uhm) a large burial place or building

motives (MOH-tivs) the goals of a person's actions

provoked (pruh-VOHKT) angered, stirred up, or enraged

summon (SUHM-uhn) to command or create

terracotta (TER-uh-KOT-uh) a hard brownish-red clay used to make sculptures

tío (TEE-oh) "uncle" in Spanish

zongzi (ZONG-zoo) a traditional sticky rice dumpling

INDEX